# THE
# BUILDING BLOCKS
# OF MEDITATION
# JOURNAL:

Sharpening Your Skills of Observation

**Nick Keomahavong**

CO-WRITTEN AND EDITED BY
Venerable Michael Viradhammo


COVER ART BY
Venerable Tim Dhiranando


DESIGNED AND ORGANIZED BY
Emmy Boonsakulcharoen

# TABLE OF CONTENTS

# MY MEDITATION TOOLBOX

## mind wandering

# MY MEDITATION TOOLBOX

sleepiness

# MY MEDITATION TOOLBOX

tension

# MY MEDITATION TOOLBOX

miscellaneous

# INTRODUCTION

## The Importance of Meditation Journaling

The purpose of this journal is to give you a supplementary workbook to help you practice and deeply integrate the information covered in the book *The Building Blocks of Meditation: The Purpose of Meditation and How to Create a Daily Practice That Actually Sticks.* The meditation guidance found in *that* book will directly correlate to the structure and content of *this* journal. This pair of resources is specifically designed to give you the proper balance of conceptual knowledge and practical stepwork to help you continuously progress on your meditation journey.

However, with that being said, if you are already a meditation practitioner, you can still use this journal by itself and benefit greatly from it. Although recommended, it is not absolutely necessary to read the first book in order for this journal to be an effective tool that helps deepen your existing practice.

Now, you might be thinking to yourself, "A meditation journal sounds a bit surfacey and superficial. Is it really going to help my meditation that much?" And the answer to that question is a resounding yes. Not only can I say this confidently from my own personal experience, but it is also echoed in the teachings of my meditation masters and tutors.

To help you understand why it is so helpful, we can compare meditation journaling to athletes watching film of their competitions. All athletes—whether their craft is football, martial arts, dance, track and field, et cetera—can greatly improve their skills if they watch film of themselves competing. In the heat of competition, athletes simply are not able to dissect each aspect of their performance, nor are they even able to be fully aware of everything that happens moment to moment.

So, when things go wrong, it can be difficult for them to understand the exact reason why. The same goes for when things go right. As a result, when the competition is over, it can be difficult for the athlete to understand—or even remember—all of the things that led to a good or bad performance.

However, watching film can help them to fill in those gaps of understanding. As they review each moment of action, they can see the big picture much more clearly. They can identify patterns much more easily. They get a better understanding of what went well and what could be improved. They now even have the option to watch film together with a coach or another experienced athlete to get some feedback on their technique.

Watching film can create a positive feedback loop of continuous improvement. Perform. Record. Analyze. Adjust. Perform better. And repeat. In essence, we could say that reviewing film is an invaluable tool that allows athletes to sharpen their skills of observation and, by extension, their level of mastery in their craft.

A meditation journal functions in much the same way. There are countless factors that can affect the quality of our meditation. So, if we don't take the time to sit down, document, and review our practice, we might spend years repeating patterns that keep us from experiencing true stillness of mind. Meditation without journaling then becomes a bit of a guessing game. We aren't so clear about what contributed to a still or "not-so-still" meditation.

This lack of clarity can lead to sporadic results and a fair amount of frustration, even if you happen to meditate daily. Despite remembering that you had a good meditation last Monday, can you remember the specific steps that led to this good experience a mere few days later? Probably not with much accuracy.

This is why the advanced meditators in our temple always advise us to write at least one journal entry per day when we enter a meditation retreat program. In these journal entries, we reflect on each experience and ask questions such as: What did I do to adjust my body and mind before and during my meditation? What obstacles did I experience? How did I overcome them? And so on. Regardless of whether it was a challenging or effortless session, noting what happened helps you tremendously.

This type of daily journaling practice clearly exposes the reality that every meditation session is different. Fluctuations in your mood, the atmosphere, your energy level, what happened to you before the session—to name just a few things—can lead to experiencing either slightly or drastically different obstacles from session to session. And, naturally, it will take some time to understand cause and effect clearly.

But over time—after you build a small catalog of entries—the patterns will start to emerge. You might start to see that "Ahhh, whenever

I drink a coffee before meditation, I get restless and my mind is too active" or "Ohhh, my best meditations are in the evening after I do ten minutes of yoga and repeat a mantra slowly and steadily."

You will gain a progressively more clear understanding of your own unique nuances regarding how to adjust your body and mind properly to discover and maintain stillness. This type of knowledge is the key to progressing in your practice. And no conceptual book can give you such individualized information. Rather, you must discover it for yourself by observing and documenting your own experience properly.

And this journal is specifically designed to help you do just that in a simple yet profound way. It will help you extract the wisdom from your direct experience and craft a personalized roadmap to deeper and more effortless meditation. And like an athlete analyzing film and then adjusting their technique accordingly, this journal will be an invaluable tool that empowers continuous improvement in your meditation. And how exactly does this journal achieve such a goal? Glad you asked.

## Journal Structure

### *Meditation Toolbox*

This journal will be broken up into various sections. As you have likely already seen after flipping through the first few pages, there are four pages at the very beginning with the heading "My Meditation Toolbox" with a specific heading underneath.

The purpose of this toolbox is to consolidate all of your best practices into a short, well-organized list. This will enable you to quickly and conveniently reference and review your own personalized list of methods that have proven effective in stilling the mind. The structure of this four-page toolbox will enable you to scan its compartments quickly and discover the tools that have helped you overcome specific obstacles in the past.

The toolbox is divided into four compartments that occupy one page each. Three of these four compartments correspond to each of the three most common obstacles that people face in meditation. The general idea is that anytime you discover a method that helps you overcome mind wandering, sleepiness, or tension, you can briefly summarize that tool in the appropriate compartment. The fourth compartment will be the place where you can store any miscellaneous methods that are not necessarily related to a specific obstacle.

In order to give you an idea of what this toolbox can look like, there will be a sample toolbox that we have prefilled that follows this introduction. Feel free to try out some of these methods in your own practice and add them to your toolbox at the beginning of this journal if they help you.

As you continue to practice meditation and discover methods that work for you, you will have the raw materials necessary to fill up each compartment. Your toolbox will become progressively more powerful as a result. Then, instead of trying to sift through the details of countless entries to discover a solution to a roadblock you are currently facing in your meditation, you can simply reference this section and easily find what you're looking for.

Return to your toolbox whenever you feel stagnant in your practice and it will present you with the know-how to get unstuck. By building and reviewing this section often, you will become like a skilled worker with the mind. You can swiftly and confidently filter through your tools until you find one that helps you achieve stillness in any situation.

## Ideas of What You Can Observe

The section that follows the sample toolbox will include a detailed list providing many of the various aspects of your practice that you can observe. The different categories included in this list mimic the structure of the blank journal pages that you will use to make your entries. Although this list will help give you many ideas of how you can observe your meditation, please keep in mind that it is not necessary to take note of all of these details each time you journal.

Rather, this is just an extensive list to draw inspiration from as you start your journaling practice. As you build on this over time, you will find your own style and rhythm. The reality is, you can journal in whatever way resonates with you. To show you a few different forms that journal entries can take, we provided you with some samples to reference.

## Sample Journal Entries

The next section of this journal will provide you with three separate sample journal entries that provide you with a range of examples from very detailed to very minimal entries. These entries will give you three ideas of how you can adjust the structure of your journal and the amount of detail that you can include, among other things.

On the note of adjusting the structure, you will notice that two of the sample entries cross out the name of one journal category and name it something more fitting for that specific session. This is one example of how you can adjust the existing structure of the journal pages to fit your own preferences.

Similar to the previous section, these are just models to give you a starting point. Feel free to get as creative as you would like and copy and develop from these entries into a system that works best for you. Once you make multiple entries, you will be able to settle into your own unique rhythm and structure.

### Connect With an Accountability Partner

The next section provides you with an extremely powerful way to enrich both your meditation and your journaling practice: finding an accountability partner. Having an individual who is implementing the habit of both meditating and journaling alongside you is extremely beneficial. You can go on this journey together and support each other through the ups, downs, and in-betweens of your practice. If a friend or family member wants to go on this journey with you, then this section will give you some ideas on how to best support each other.

But what happens if you don't have a friend or family member who wants to establish this meditation habit alongside you? Have no fear! We have already thought about this and have a great solution for you. There will be a QR code in this section that will take you to a section of our online Reddit community. This will be a place where people such as yourself who are looking for accountability partners can convene and partner up to provide mutual support on this meditative journey.

### Clarify Your Why

The second to last section before you reach the blank journal pages will help you clarify your "why." Getting clear on the most powerful reasons why you want to create and maintain a meditation habit is a very beneficial exercise both at the beginning and along the way of your meditation journey. At first, there will most likely be some resistance and struggles as you seek to incorporate this behavior change into your daily life. And there will also likely be rough patches in your practice where you don't feel so motivated to sit. So having a one-page sheet of your deepest motivations for practicing can be an easy way to reconnect with a powerful source of internal motivation.

### Favorite Sessions

With a similar objective, the section that follows will give you a place to make note of the highlights, the rating, and the page number of your favorite meditation sessions so you can reconnect with them easily. This section will also include an explanation of the rating system so you can understand how it can help your journaling practice. Reconnecting with both your reasons for meditating and the good inner experiences you have had can help you persevere in the face of resistance. So these last two sections will guide you on how you can create such resources for yourself.

## Proper Mindset for Journaling

Before I release you into the wonderful world of journaling where you will undoubtedly craft an incredible roadmap to meditation mastery, I would like to give you two last pieces of advice. These tips will help you adopt the appropriate mindset when approaching meditation journaling.

First of all, when journaling . . . please, be kind to yourself.

We discussed this quite a bit in the other book, but it's worth reiterating here. There will be ups and downs in your practice. There will be times—perhaps more often than not—where your mind will wander for a majority of the session. Maybe it isn't still for the whole time you are meditating. And that's ok. That is normal in the beginning and even during certain stressful or busy time periods in our life.

Journaling is not about being a harsh judge of your experience. It's not about determining whether you are a good meditator or not or whether you are better or worse than your friend. Rather, it is about sharpening your skills of observation.

And as was a central theme in the main book, the key to effective meditation and refined skills of observation is neutrality. Both inside and outside of our meditation session, we observe things neutrally. Keep in mind the perspective that there's no such thing as a "bad" meditation session, just opportunities to get a better understanding of our own mind. So, again, please be kind to yourself when journaling.

And last, but certainly not least, make sure that you have fun with this process! Get creative. Get excited. Draw pictures. Share your experience with your accountability partner. Celebrate your efforts towards implementing this wholesome habit together. Feel proud of yourself for undertaking this journey. And just approach this meditation path with a very lighthearted, not-so-serious mentality. With this approach and the guidance provided in this journal and book set, I am confident you will have an inredibly transformative and enjoyable experience. :)

## Bonus Gift

Oh ya! Before you get started, let me mention one last thing. Some people might really connect with this concept of journaling but find it difficult to always have this physical book handy each time they want to journal. If you are one of those people, don't worry ... we've got you covered! My team and I have created an electronic version of the meditation toolbox, journal entries, and other select sections of this journal that you can download for free from my website. This fillable PDF can be downloaded to your device so that you can type your entries and store it electronically. Pretty neat, huh? We thought so too.

If you would like to download this e-journal, then please scan the QR code or visit the link shown below. We hope you enjoy!

 QR code and link for free download
https://nickkeomahavong.com/ejournal

# SAMPLE TOOLBOX

## mind wandering

- Mantra: "Samma Arahang"
- Mantra: "Let It Go"
- Mantra: "Clear and Bright"
- Repeating mantra more slowly
- Repeating mantra more quickly
- Opening my eyes very slightly then reclosing them
- Fluttering my eyelids
- Taking a deep breath
- Observing the rise and fall of my stomach as I breathe
- Adjusting my sitting position
- Placing my mind more gently on the meditation tool
- Allowing my mind to wander for a little bit and then opening my eyes to reset
- Journaling/braindumping outside of session for heavy emotions
- Opening my eyes and allowing emotion to fade
- Change my perspective from wanting to meditate well or wanting my mind to be still to just observing neutrally
- Repeating mantra: "Neutral, Neutral, Neutral"
- Noting technique: Observing thoughts neutrally and removing emotions/stories from them outside of the session

# SAMPLE TOOLBOX

## sleepiness

- Opening my eyes and looking at something bright
- Keeping my eyes open until the sleepiness fades
- Taking a few deep breaths
- Holding my breath on the inhale for ten seconds
- Focusing on my breath and counting the exhale up to ten and then restarting
- Getting up to go to the bathroom and wash my face
- Drinking some water
- Walking meditation
- Stretching
- Taking a quick nap before meditation (less than 30 min)
- Drinking some coffee before meditation
- Doing some light exercise before meditation
- Taking a shower before meditation
- Changing my posture to be more upright so I am not leaning against anything

# SAMPLE TOOLBOX

## tension

- Yoga before session
- Stretching while sitting down in session
- Simply observing the tension neutrally like it is my meditation tool and watching it eventually fade away
- Walking meditation
- Slight adjustments of my sitting position
- Adding more support with pillows or rolled-up blankets wherever I need it
- Relaxing the muscles in my face
- Rubbing my hands together to generate heat and then holding them over my eyes to relax them
- Facial massage
- When I feel too focused, I expand my awareness to surround my whole body like I'm sitting in a bubble
- I let go of all mental tools and just try to fall asleep sitting up

# SAMPLE TOOLBOX

## miscellaneous

- Going for a walk before I meditate
- Listening to guided meditations
- Listening to nature sounds on a meditation app
- Lighting candles
- Saying a prayer to my favorite spiritual figures asking for guidance before meditating
- Thinking of the good deeds I have done before meditating
- Spreading feelings of loving kindness like an expanding bubble to all beings
- Spreading feelings of loving kindness to those I love, feel neutral towards, and have negative emotions towards
- Short exercise before sitting to be alert and then just trying to fall asleep sitting up

# IDEAS FOR WHAT YOU CAN OBSERVE

The following categories give you some ideas of how to make note of the many things you can observe before and during your meditation session. The goal is not to write a perfect entry each time but rather to discover a way of journaling that is beneficial and sustainable for you.

## Basics:

**Date, Time, Duration, Location:** The date is always nice to track to see how your practice progresses over time. Making note of the time can help reveal how each time of day affects the readiness of your mind to meditate. Journaling the duration of your practice can help you tune into the ideal length of time to practice. Finally, location can help you identify which setting is most conducive to your stillness of mind.

## Before Session:

**Food, Water, and Rest:** Did you eat mindfully? Too much or too little? Was it healthy? Did you eat too fast? Were you hydrated enough? Did you get enough sleep from the night before? (*Hint: Finding balance in these categories can help overcome sleepiness in meditation*)

**Adjusting Body and Mind:** Did you take any measures to relax your body/mind (*e.g., stretching, yoga, deep breathing, recollecting good deeds, walking in nature*)? Were you rushing to get to the session on time? Were you talking about things that help or hinder neutrality of mind?

**Emotions:** What was your mood like? Were you able to maintain positive or neutral emotions during your daily activities? Did you do any activities to flush emotions before sitting (*e.g., exercise, journaling, Qi Gong*)?

## During Session:

**Techniques**: What steps did you take to create and maintain body and mind comfort (*e.g. sitting position, listening to guidance/nature sounds/silence*)? What meditation technique did you use (*e.g., mantra, visualization, awareness at center, awareness of breath, doing nothing, etc.*)? Was it effective?

**Obstacles:** What obstacles did you face (*e.g., sleepiness, tension, mind wandering*)? Observe how these are related to the things you did before the session. What steps did you take to correct them (*e.g., opening eyes, adjusting body, deep breaths*)? How effective were these corrections?

**Inner Experiences:** Describe any images, brightness, sensations (*e.g., falling, expanding, shrinking, etc.*), or feelings (*e.g., stillness, bliss, contentment, etc.*) that you experienced.

## Draw a Picture:

# SAMPLE
# JOURNAL ENTRIES

When journaling, some people really want to dig deep and pick apart each aspect of their practice in-depth. These types of detail-oriented people can reference the lengthy sample journal below for ideas of what things to observe and how to make note of them.

However, those who prefer something quick and simple might feel overwhelmed by merely looking at the intricacy of the detailed entry. And this is why we also show a sample that is extremely minimal. Journal entries on either side or in the middle of the spectrum will be just fine. There is no right or wrong. No better or worse.

Really, at the end of the day, it's all about what works for you. If you want to illustrate it, graph things, cross out the categories provided and make new ones, or anything in between, feel free to get creative and make it your own.

The most important thing is that you journal consistently. As addressed in the introduction, these samples just give you three very diverse models to inspire your journaling as well as impressing upon you that you can journal in any way that you like and find beneficial. Adjust whenever needed, and, as always, just have fun with the process!

# DETAILED JOURNAL ENTRY

| Location | Time & Duration | Date |
|---|---|---|
| Back Porch | 7:30 a.m. – 8:15 a.m. = 45 mins | 10 Feb 2022 |

| Rating | Key Takeaways |
|---|---|
| 4.5/5 stars | Yoga + Coffee = good prep. Don't rush to close your eyes. No expectations = stillness of mind. |

**Before Session**

Body/Mind Prep: I had a cup of coffee, a glass of water, and did about 10 minutes of yoga before sitting. This helped to energize my body and mind. But it ended up being too much liquid, because I had to go to the bathroom in the middle of my session (maybe drink less water, because coffee helped). I also kept my phone in airplane mode overnight and didn't turn it off until after my meditation. This really helped reduce mind wandering (add to toolbox).

**During Session**

Techniques: I started off my meditation by keeping my eyes open for a little while to look at the flowers on my porch as I focused on my breath. Once my mind became relaxed, I closed my eyes softly and started to repeat the mantra "Samma Arahang." It seemed to help to repeat "Samma" on the in breath and "Arahang" on the out breath.

Obstacles: My session started off very well. My mind became calm and a very pleasant sensation arose in my stomach after about 10 minutes. But when I tried to focus more on this sensation, it disappeared and I felt some tension and tightness in my forehead. Then about 25 minutes into my meditation, I had to get up to go to the bathroom.

Inner Experiences: After coming back from the bathroom, I didn't expect much to happen for the last 10–15 minutes before my alarm went off. But, surprisingly, my mind became very still. My body started to become light and my hands started to feel like they were disappearing. I felt very peaceful and content.

# MODERATE JOURNAL ENTRY

| Location | Time & Duration | Date |
|----------|-----------------|------|
| My Car | 20 min on lunch break | March 27 |

| Rating | Key Takeaways |
|--------|---------------|
| 4.7/5 | |

~~Before Session~~  Key Takeaways

Listening to nature sounds with earbuds and imagining I'm in nature helps A LOT. It takes my mind about 10 minutes to get settled.

During Session

I noticed on the last lunch break when I meditated in my car in a shady parking spot that the sound of the cars disturbed my peace of mind. So, I put in earbuds and listened to the sound of a river with a meditation app. This not only blocked out the distractions that surrounded me but it also made me feel like I was in nature. I closed my eyes and just imagined I was alone in the forest where I like to go camping. I visualized the sun coming through the trees and warming my body. My mind wandered a little bit in the first 10 minutes, but I was able to bring it back to this feeling of being in the sunlight in nature. Time passed by quickly and I felt very refreshed afterwards as I headed back into work.

# MINIMAL JOURNAL ENTRY

| Location | Time & Duration | Date |
|---|---|---|
| | 5 — 10 min | April 22 |

| Rating | Key Takeaways |
|---|---|
| | |

~~Before~~ Session
After

During Session

I meditated before bed by repeating the mantra "Calm and Relaxed." It really helped me prepare for bed, let go of the problems of the day, and led to a good night's sleep. Feel proud that I kept my habit even after a busy day.

# CONNECT WITH AN ACCOUNTABILITY PARTNER

As stated in the introduction, having an accountability partner is extremely beneficial, especially while attempting to implement a new habit. If a friend or family member wants to go on this journey with you, then this section will give you some ideas on how to best support each other. But if none of your loved ones are up for the task, you can scan the QR code or follow the link below to get access to a post on our online Reddit community dedicated to helping people such as yourself connect with an accountability partner.

## Ideas for Accountability Partners:

- Decide how often/when you will meet up/discuss your experiences.
- Share your goals with each other.
- Discuss the reasons why you both want to build this habit.
- Share inspirational words or quotes to motivate each other.
- Share/ask about techniques that have been effective.
- Share what things you have found are helpful to avoid in order to meditate more effectively.
- Share/ask about your favorite journaling formats or techniques.
- Share/ask what accessories/seats/locations have been helpful for your body and mind.

- Share/ask what time of day works best and why.
- Share/ask what things you do to prepare well for meditation.
- Share/ask what types of resources/apps/guided meditations have helped.

 QR code and link to access Reddit post:
https://nickkeomahavong.com/meditation-1

# CLARIFY YOUR WHY

Take some time now to brainstorm and get clear on some of the powerful reasons why you are incorporating meditation into your life. Then go ahead and jot them down on the next page, on a separate piece of paper, or on the printable template from the QR code or link provided below. Once you feel like you have listed a few strong points, keep this in a prominent place where you can reconnect with that internal source of motivation to keep staying consistent in this transformative practice. Feel free to add more reasons to this list as you progress on your journey and experience new positive benefits in your life.

 QR code and link to access printable templates:
https://nickkeomahavong.com/meditation-1

# CLARIFY YOUR WHY

Why is a meditation practice important to you?

# FAVORITE SESSIONS

Adding your favorite sessions to the next page can help you easily reference an inspirational session when you need a little encouragement and motivation to meditate. This page will serve as a reminder of how meditation has made you feel.

A note about the rating category found here and in the blank journal entries: It is not prompting you to judge your experience as good or bad. Rather, its purpose is to help you easily find the entries for "stiller" meditations and identify the steps they have in common both before and during the meditation. This will clue you in on which things to repeat. It will also help you do the same with the "not-so-still" experiences so you can see what to avoid. Keep in mind, there is no such thing as a bad meditation, only opportunities to hone in on your most effective method to stillness in all situations.

# FAVORITE SESSIONS

| Page | Rating | Highlights |
|------|--------|-----------|
|      |        |           |

# SUMMARY OF STEPS TO GET STARTED

1. Meditate.

2. Write about your experience.

3. If you found a tool that worked, add it to the master sheet.

4. Take a moment to feel proud of a job well done.

5. (Optional but recommended) Chat with your accountability partner to either motivate, support, get feedback, or just discuss your meditation journey together.

# HAPPY

# JOURNALING!

# JOURNAL ENTRY

| Location | Time & Duration | Date |
|----------|-----------------|------|
| Rating | Key Takeaways | |

Before Session

During Session

# JOURNAL ENTRY

| Location | Time & Duration | Date |
|----------|-----------------|------|
| Rating | Key Takeaways | |

## Before Session

## During Session

# JOURNAL ENTRY

| Location | Time & Duration | Date |
|----------|-----------------|------|
| Rating | Key Takeaways | |

**Before Session**

**During Session**

# JOURNAL ENTRY

| Location | Time & Duration | Date |
|----------|-----------------|------|
| Rating | Key Takeaways | |

**Before Session**

**During Session**

# JOURNAL ENTRY

| Location | Time & Duration | Date |
|----------|-----------------|------|
| Rating | Key Takeaways | |

**Before Session**

**During Session**

# JOURNAL ENTRY

| Location | Time & Duration | Date |
|----------|-----------------|------|
| Rating | Key Takeaways | |

Before Session

During Session

# JOURNAL ENTRY

| Location | Time & Duration | Date |
|---|---|---|
| Rating | Key Takeaways | |

**Before Session**

**During Session**

# JOURNAL ENTRY

| Location | Time & Duration | Date |
|---|---|---|
| Rating | Key Takeaways | |

**Before Session**

**During Session**

# JOURNAL ENTRY

| Location | Time & Duration | Date |
|----------|-----------------|------|
| Rating | Key Takeaways | |

Before Session

During Session

# JOURNAL ENTRY

| Location | Time & Duration | Date |
|----------|-----------------|------|
| Rating | Key Takeaways | |

Before Session

During Session

# JOURNAL ENTRY

| Location | Time & Duration | Date |
|----------|-----------------|------|
| Rating | Key Takeaways | |

**Before Session**

**During Session**

# JOURNAL ENTRY

| Location | Time & Duration | Date |
|----------|-----------------|------|
| Rating | Key Takeaways | |

Before Session

During Session

# JOURNAL ENTRY

| Location | Time & Duration | Date |
|----------|-----------------|------|
| Rating | Key Takeaways | |

Before Session

During Session

# JOURNAL ENTRY

| Location | Time & Duration | Date |
|----------|-----------------|------|
| Rating | Key Takeaways | |

**Before Session**

**During Session**

# JOURNAL ENTRY

| Location | Time & Duration | Date |
|----------|-----------------|------|
| Rating | Key Takeaways | |

**Before Session**

**During Session**

# JOURNAL ENTRY

| Location | Time & Duration | Date |
|----------|-----------------|------|
| Rating | Key Takeaways | |

**Before Session**

**During Session**

# JOURNAL ENTRY

| Location | Time & Duration | Date |
|---|---|---|
| Rating | Key Takeaways | |

**Before Session**

**During Session**

# JOURNAL ENTRY

| Location | Time & Duration | Date |
|----------|-----------------|------|
| Rating | Key Takeaways | |

**Before Session**

**During Session**

# JOURNAL ENTRY

| Location | Time & Duration | Date |
|---|---|---|
| Rating | Key Takeaways | |

Before Session

During Session

# JOURNAL ENTRY

| Location | Time & Duration | Date |
|----------|-----------------|------|
| Rating | Key Takeaways | |

Before Session

During Session

# JOURNAL ENTRY

| Location | Time & Duration | Date |
|----------|-----------------|------|
| Rating | Key Takeaways | |

Before Session

During Session

# JOURNAL ENTRY

| Location | Time & Duration | Date |
|---|---|---|
| Rating | Key Takeaways | |

**Before Session**

**During Session**

# JOURNAL ENTRY

| Location | Time & Duration | Date |
|----------|----------------|------|
| Rating | Key Takeaways | |

Before Session

During Session

# JOURNAL ENTRY

| Location | Time & Duration | Date |
|----------|-----------------|------|
| Rating | Key Takeaways | |

Before Session

During Session

# JOURNAL ENTRY

| Location | Time & Duration | Date |
|---|---|---|
| Rating | Key Takeaways | |

Before Session

During Session

# JOURNAL ENTRY

| Location | Time & Duration | Date |
|----------|-----------------|------|
| Rating | Key Takeaways | |

**Before Session**

**During Session**

# JOURNAL ENTRY

| Location | Time & Duration | Date |
|----------|-----------------|------|
| Rating | Key Takeaways | |

**Before Session**

**During Session**

# JOURNAL ENTRY

| Location | Time & Duration | Date |
|----------|-----------------|------|
| Rating | Key Takeaways | |

## Before Session

## During Session

# JOURNAL ENTRY

| Location | Time & Duration | Date |
|----------|-----------------|------|
| Rating | Key Takeaways | |

## Before Session

## During Session

# JOURNAL ENTRY

| Location | Time & Duration | Date |
|----------|-----------------|------|
| Rating | Key Takeaways | |

Before Session

During Session

# JOURNAL ENTRY

| Location | Time & Duration | Date |
|----------|-----------------|------|
| Rating | Key Takeaways | |

**Before Session**

**During Session**

# JOURNAL ENTRY

| Location | Time & Duration | Date |
|----------|-----------------|------|
| Rating | Key Takeaways | |

Before Session

During Session

# JOURNAL ENTRY

| Location | Time & Duration | Date |
|----------|-----------------|------|
| Rating | Key Takeaways | |

Before Session

During Session

# JOURNAL ENTRY

| Location | Time & Duration | Date |
|----------|-----------------|------|
| Rating | Key Takeaways | |

**Before Session**

**During Session**

# JOURNAL ENTRY

| Location | Time & Duration | Date |
|----------|-----------------|------|
| Rating | Key Takeaways | |

Before Session

During Session

# JOURNAL ENTRY

| Location | Time & Duration | Date |
|---|---|---|
| Rating | Key Takeaways | |

**Before Session**

**During Session**

# JOURNAL ENTRY

| Location | Time & Duration | Date |
|----------|-----------------|------|
| Rating | Key Takeaways | |

**Before Session**

**During Session**

# JOURNAL ENTRY

| Location | Time & Duration | Date |
|----------|-----------------|------|
| Rating | Key Takeaways | |

**Before Session**

**During Session**

# JOURNAL ENTRY

| Location | Time & Duration | Date |
|----------|-----------------|------|
| Rating | Key Takeaways | |

**Before Session**

**During Session**

# JOURNAL ENTRY

| Location | Time & Duration | Date |
|----------|-----------------|------|
| Rating | Key Takeaways | |

Before Session

During Session

# JOURNAL ENTRY

| Location | Time & Duration | Date |
|----------|-----------------|------|
| Rating | Key Takeaways | |

**Before Session**

**During Session**

# JOURNAL ENTRY

| Location | Time & Duration | Date |
|---|---|---|
| Rating | Key Takeaways | |

**Before Session**

**During Session**

# JOURNAL ENTRY

| Location | Time & Duration | Date |
|---|---|---|
| Rating | Key Takeaways | |

Before Session

During Session

# JOURNAL ENTRY

| Location | Time & Duration | Date |
|----------|-----------------|------|
| Rating | Key Takeaways | |

**Before Session**

**During Session**

# JOURNAL ENTRY

| Location | Time & Duration | Date |
|----------|-----------------|------|
| Rating | Key Takeaways | |

Before Session

During Session

# JOURNAL ENTRY

| Location | Time & Duration | Date |
|----------|-----------------|------|
| Rating | Key Takeaways | |

**Before Session**

**During Session**

# JOURNAL ENTRY

| Location | Time & Duration | Date |
|----------|-----------------|------|
| Rating | Key Takeaways | |

**Before Session**

**During Session**

# JOURNAL ENTRY

| Location | Time & Duration | Date |
|---|---|---|
| Rating | Key Takeaways | |

**Before Session**

**During Session**

# JOURNAL ENTRY

| Location | Time & Duration | Date |
|---|---|---|
| Rating | Key Takeaways | |

Before Session

During Session

# JOURNAL ENTRY

| Location | Time & Duration | Date |
|---|---|---|
| Rating | Key Takeaways | |

## Before Session

## During Session

# JOURNAL ENTRY

| Location | Time & Duration | Date |
|----------|-----------------|------|
| Rating | Key Takeaways | |

**Before Session**

**During Session**

# JOURNAL ENTRY

| Location | Time & Duration | Date |
|----------|-----------------|------|
| Rating | Key Takeaways | |

## Before Session

## During Session

# JOURNAL ENTRY

| Location | Time & Duration | Date |
|---|---|---|
| Rating | Key Takeaways | |

**Before Session**

**During Session**

# JOURNAL ENTRY

| Location | Time & Duration | Date |
|----------|-----------------|------|
| Rating | Key Takeaways | |

**Before Session**

**During Session**

# JOURNAL ENTRY

| Location | Time & Duration | Date |
|----------|-----------------|------|
| Rating | Key Takeaways | |

**Before Session**

**During Session**

# JOURNAL ENTRY

| Location | Time & Duration | Date |
|----------|-----------------|------|
| Rating | Key Takeaways | |

**Before Session**

**During Session**

# JOURNAL ENTRY

| Location | Time & Duration | Date |
|----------|-----------------|------|
| Rating | Key Takeaways | |

Before Session

During Session

# JOURNAL ENTRY

| Location | Time & Duration | Date |
|----------|-----------------|------|
| Rating | Key Takeaways | |

Before Session

During Session

# JOURNAL ENTRY

| Location | Time & Duration | Date |
|----------|-----------------|------|
| Rating | Key Takeaways | |

**Before Session**

**During Session**

# JOURNAL ENTRY

| Location | Time & Duration | Date |
|----------|-----------------|------|
| Rating | Key Takeaways | |

Before Session

During Session

# JOURNAL ENTRY

| Location | Time & Duration | Date |
|----------|-----------------|------|
| Rating | Key Takeaways | |

**Before Session**

**During Session**

# JOURNAL ENTRY

| Location | Time & Duration | Date |
|----------|-----------------|------|
| Rating | Key Takeaways | |

**Before Session**

**During Session**

# JOURNAL ENTRY

| Location | Time & Duration | Date |
|----------|-----------------|------|
| Rating | Key Takeaways | |

**Before Session**

**During Session**

# JOURNAL ENTRY

| Location | Time & Duration | Date |
|----------|-----------------|------|
| Rating | Key Takeaways | |

## Before Session

## During Session

# JOURNAL ENTRY

| Location | Time & Duration | Date |
|----------|----------------|------|
| Rating | Key Takeaways | |

**Before Session**

**During Session**

# JOURNAL ENTRY

| Location | Time & Duration | Date |
|----------|-----------------|------|
| Rating | Key Takeaways | |

**Before Session**

**During Session**

# JOURNAL ENTRY

| Location | Time & Duration | Date |
|----------|-----------------|------|
| Rating | Key Takeaways | |

**Before Session**

**During Session**

# JOURNAL ENTRY

| Location | Time & Duration | Date |
|----------|-----------------|------|
| Rating | Key Takeaways | |

**Before Session**

**During Session**

# JOURNAL ENTRY

| Location | Time & Duration | Date |
|---|---|---|
| Rating | Key Takeaways | |

**Before Session**

**During Session**

# JOURNAL ENTRY

| Location | Time & Duration | Date |
|----------|-----------------|------|
| Rating | Key Takeaways | |

**Before Session**

**During Session**

# JOURNAL ENTRY

| Location | Time & Duration | Date |
|----------|-----------------|------|
| Rating | Key Takeaways | |

## Before Session

## During Session

# JOURNAL ENTRY

| Location | Time & Duration | Date |
|---|---|---|
| Rating | Key Takeaways | |

**Before Session**

**During Session**

# JOURNAL ENTRY

| Location | Time & Duration | Date |
|----------|-----------------|------|
| Rating | Key Takeaways | |

**Before Session**



**During Session**

# JOURNAL ENTRY

| Location | Time & Duration | Date |
|----------|-----------------|------|
| Rating | Key Takeaways | |

**Before Session**

**During Session**

# JOURNAL ENTRY

| Location | Time & Duration | Date |
|----------|-----------------|------|
| Rating | Key Takeaways | |

Before Session

During Session

# JOURNAL ENTRY

| Location | Time & Duration | Date |
|----------|-----------------|------|
| Rating | Key Takeaways | |

## Before Session

## During Session

# JOURNAL ENTRY

| Location | Time & Duration | Date |
|---|---|---|
| Rating | Key Takeaways | |

**Before Session**

**During Session**

# JOURNAL ENTRY

| Location | Time & Duration | Date |
|----------|-----------------|------|
| Rating | Key Takeaways | |

**Before Session**

**During Session**

# JOURNAL ENTRY

| Location | Time & Duration | Date |
|----------|-----------------|------|
| Rating | Key Takeaways | |

**Before Session**

**During Session**

# JOURNAL ENTRY

| Location | Time & Duration | Date |
|----------|-----------------|------|
| Rating | Key Takeaways | |

**Before Session**

**During Session**

# JOURNAL ENTRY

| Location | Time & Duration | Date |
|----------|-----------------|------|
| Rating | Key Takeaways | |

**Before Session**

**During Session**

# JOURNAL ENTRY

| Location | Time & Duration | Date |
|----------|-----------------|------|
| Rating | Key Takeaways | |

**Before Session**

**During Session**

# JOURNAL ENTRY

| Location | Time & Duration | Date |
|----------|-----------------|------|
| Rating | Key Takeaways | |

Before Session

During Session

# JOURNAL ENTRY

| Location | Time & Duration | Date |
|----------|-----------------|------|
| Rating | Key Takeaways | |

**Before Session**

**During Session**

# JOURNAL ENTRY

| Location | Time & Duration | Date |
|---|---|---|
| Rating | Key Takeaways | |

**Before Session**

**During Session**

# JOURNAL ENTRY

| Location | Time & Duration | Date |
|----------|-----------------|------|
| Rating | Key Takeaways | |

**Before Session**

**During Session**

# JOURNAL ENTRY

| Location | Time & Duration | Date |
|---|---|---|
| Rating | Key Takeaways | |

**Before Session**

**During Session**

# JOURNAL ENTRY

| Location | Time & Duration | Date |
|---|---|---|
| Rating | Key Takeaways | |

Before Session

During Session

# JOURNAL ENTRY

| Location | Time & Duration | Date |
|---|---|---|
| Rating | Key Takeaways | |

**Before Session**

**During Session**

# JOURNAL ENTRY

| Location | Time & Duration | Date |
|---|---|---|
| Rating | Key Takeaways | |

**Before Session**

**During Session**

# JOURNAL ENTRY

| Location | Time & Duration | Date |
|----------|-----------------|------|
| Rating | Key Takeaways | |

**Before Session**

**During Session**

# JOURNAL ENTRY

| Location | Time & Duration | Date |
|----------|-----------------|------|
| Rating | Key Takeaways | |

## Before Session

## During Session

# JOURNAL ENTRY

| Location | Time & Duration | Date |
|----------|-----------------|------|
| Rating | Key Takeaways | |

**Before Session**

**During Session**

# JOURNAL ENTRY

| Location | Time & Duration | Date |
|---|---|---|
| Rating | Key Takeaways | |

**Before Session**

**During Session**

# JOURNAL ENTRY

| Location | Time & Duration | Date |
|----------|-----------------|------|
| Rating | Key Takeaways | |

Before Session

During Session

# JOURNAL ENTRY

| Location | Time & Duration | Date |
|----------|-----------------|------|
| Rating | Key Takeaways | |

**Before Session**

**During Session**

# JOURNAL ENTRY

| Location | Time & Duration | Date |
|----------|-----------------|------|
| Rating | Key Takeaways | |

**Before Session**

**During Session**

# JOURNAL ENTRY

| Location | Time & Duration | Date |
|----------|-----------------|------|
| Rating | Key Takeaways | |

## Before Session

## During Session

# JOURNAL ENTRY

| Location | Time & Duration | Date |
|----------|-----------------|------|
| Rating | Key Takeaways | |

Before Session

During Session

# JOURNAL ENTRY

| Location | Time & Duration | Date |
|----------|-----------------|------|
| Rating | Key Takeaways | |

## Before Session

## During Session

# JOURNAL ENTRY

| Location | Time & Duration | Date |
|----------|-----------------|------|
| Rating | Key Takeaways | |

## Before Session

## During Session

# JOURNAL ENTRY

| Location | Time & Duration | Date |
|---|---|---|
| Rating | Key Takeaways | |

**Before Session**

**During Session**

# JOURNAL ENTRY

| Location | Time & Duration | Date |
|---|---|---|
| Rating | Key Takeaways | |

### Before Session

### During Session

# JOURNAL ENTRY

| Location | Time & Duration | Date |
|----------|-----------------|------|
| Rating | Key Takeaways | |

**Before Session**

**During Session**

# JOURNAL ENTRY

| Location | Time & Duration | Date |
|----------|-----------------|------|
| Rating | Key Takeaways | |

## Before Session

## During Session

# JOURNAL ENTRY

| Location | Time & Duration | Date |
|---|---|---|
| Rating | Key Takeaways | |

**Before Session**

**During Session**

# JOURNAL ENTRY

| Location | Time & Duration | Date |
|---|---|---|
| Rating | Key Takeaways | |

**Before Session**

**During Session**

# JOURNAL ENTRY

| Location | Time & Duration | Date |
|---|---|---|
| Rating | Key Takeaways | |

### Before Session

### During Session

# JOURNAL ENTRY

| Location | Time & Duration | Date |
|----------|-----------------|------|
| Rating | Key Takeaways | |

Before Session

During Session

# JOURNAL ENTRY

| Location | Time & Duration | Date |
|---|---|---|
| Rating | Key Takeaways | |

**Before Session**

**During Session**

# JOURNAL ENTRY

| Location | Time & Duration | Date |
|----------|-----------------|------|
| Rating | Key Takeaways | |

**Before Session**

**During Session**

# JOURNAL ENTRY

| Location | Time & Duration | Date |
|---|---|---|
| Rating | Key Takeaways | |

**Before Session**

**During Session**

# JOURNAL ENTRY

| Location | Time & Duration | Date |
|----------|-----------------|------|
| Rating | Key Takeaways | |

## Before Session

## During Session

# JOURNAL ENTRY

| Location | Time & Duration | Date |
|----------|-----------------|------|
| Rating | Key Takeaways | |

**Before Session**

**During Session**

# JOURNAL ENTRY

| Location | Time & Duration | Date |
|---|---|---|
| Rating | Key Takeaways | |

**Before Session**

**During Session**

# JOURNAL ENTRY

| Location | Time & Duration | Date |
|----------|-----------------|------|
| Rating | Key Takeaways | |

**Before Session**

**During Session**

# JOURNAL ENTRY

| Location | Time & Duration | Date |
|----------|-----------------|------|
| Rating | Key Takeaways | |

**Before Session**

**During Session**

# JOURNAL ENTRY

| Location | Time & Duration | Date |
|----------|-----------------|------|
| Rating | Key Takeaways | |

Before Session

During Session

# JOURNAL ENTRY

| Location | Time & Duration | Date |
|----------|-----------------|------|
| Rating | Key Takeaways | |

**Before Session**

**During Session**

# JOURNAL ENTRY

| Location | Time & Duration | Date |
|----------|-----------------|------|
| Rating | Key Takeaways | |

**Before Session**

**During Session**

# JOURNAL ENTRY

| Location | Time & Duration | Date |
|----------|-----------------|------|
| Rating | Key Takeaways | |

Before Session

During Session

# JOURNAL ENTRY

| Location | Time & Duration | Date |
|----------|-----------------|------|
| Rating | Key Takeaways | |

Before Session

During Session

# ABOUT THE AUTHORS
## Venerable Nick Santacitto

Venerable Nick, previously a practicing psychotherapist, has been ordained as a Theravada Buddhist monk in Thailand since 2018. His books capture his unique perspective by interweaving the tools of the mental health world and the wisdom of Buddhism into simple and practical guides to healing. With a background as a YouTuber and a professional hip-hop dancer, Nick likes to keep it real and deliver his message to the reader with a refreshing, modern flavor. The directness of his writing cuts past the fluff and gets to the point in a way that is relatable and easy to connect with.

Nick has acquired a diverse range of professional experience in the mental health field over the past decade, including but not limited to: being the lead clinician at a foster home for over one hundred kids aged twelve to eighteen; being a program therapist at a drug treatment center in Malibu, California; being a bereavement counselor at a hospice; and being the founder and owner of his private practice, True Nature Counseling Center, in San Diego, California.

However, at the pinnacle of his professional success, Nick left it all behind to become a Buddhist monk in Thailand. He wanted to delve deeper into his own healing and become a more refined practitioner of the tools that he was teaching. As he fully focused his energy on becoming more deeply congruent and aligned with his true nature, his understanding of human suffering and how to heal it matured greatly. It is his highest mission to share this knowledge with others in order to help them discover their true nature and live their most authentic lives.

# ABOUT THE AUTHORS
## Venerable Michael Viradhammo

After discovering the healing power of Buddhism and meditation, Venerable Michael decided to abandon material pursuits, dropped out of university, paid back his loans, and went to ordain as a Buddhist monk in Thailand, where he has been a monk since 2017. After ordaining, Venerable Michael has spent much of his time teaching meditation and wisdom to travelers at the Pa Pae Meditation Retreat in Chiang Mai as well as teaching and mentoring men who become monks with the international ordination program.

He is also an avid writer and is pursuing his passion by cowriting books about practical wisdom to help readers overcome their suffering with his monk brother, Venerable Nick. By learning, applying, teaching, and writing Venerable Nick's unique perspective that bridges mental health with spiritual health, Venerable Michael is deeply dedicated to continuously aligning his life with his true nature and helping others do the same.

# CONNECT WITH
# THE AUTHORS

Visit Venerable Nick's website for a central place to access all of the projects that he has completed and is currently working on: https://nickkeomahavong.com/

Get a better feel for the broad range of topics, concepts, and stories that Venerable Nick has an interest in by visiting his YouTube channel: Nick Keomahavong.

Stay updated with any new resources, products, or other announce-ments by signing up for Venerable Nick's mailing list: tinyurl.com/nickkeomahavong

Join our online Reddit community where we keep the conversation going. This platform helps to foster strong spiritual friendships and instigate the discussion surrounding Venerable Nick's content. Come share your story: https://www.reddit.com/r/NickKeomahavong/